# RUN

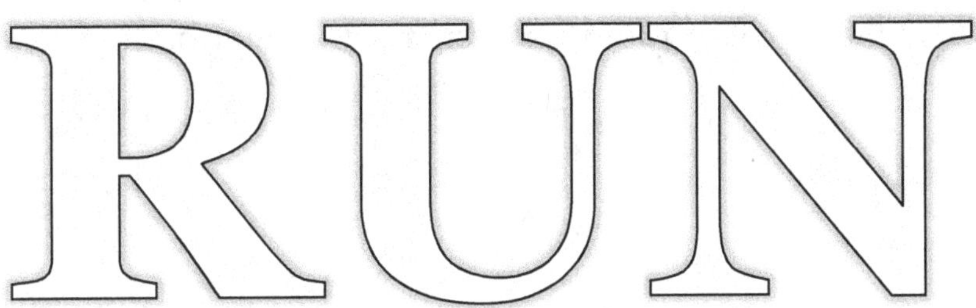

## A Road Less Traveled

*By Author*

*Joshua L. King*

# Table of Contents

# *Dedication*

To my best friend, my wife, Candi. You have always supported me from the beginning. Because of you I can. Thank you for pushing me to finish my degree. Thank you for supporting my political aspirations and thank you for keeping it real with me. You made me whole and I truly appreciate all the sacrifices that you made to make it happen.

*-Josh*

# *Acknowledgements*

I want to thank God for keeping me safe and bringing me home from the war with my mind and my body. I could not have done anything without you.

# JOSHUA KING

First, I have to say thank you to my father, Dr. Herman Lavon King (aka Pop). You have been my writing coach for years and I could not have made it this far without your strength and determination to make me be a better writer and a better person.

Thank you, Joan Jones (Ma), for raising me right and keeping me off the street. Your sacrifices will never be forgotten. I hope that I am making you proud.

I want to give a shout out to my brother, Simeon, and my sisters, Yaminah and Tacara. You are my partners, my friends, and my mentors. Thank you for telling me the truth and keeping it real.

I want to give a special thanks to the Democratic Party of Virginia for believing in me. Thank you for your support over the years. I am here to stay and I will continue to serve for as long as you need me.

Finally, I want to thank George Mason University administrators for preparing me for community service. You taught me how to express myself on paper and I am eternally grateful.

# *Preface*

I titled this book *Run, a Road Less Traveled,* because many citizens will never run for office. To run for office, you will have to sacrifice your greatest commodity, time. Most people do not control their time and can't afford to stop working to run for office.

I wrote this book because I believe that the general public needs to know about the election cycles, voting, and how to become a candidate.

What motivated me to write this book was the fact that I was not taught about local politics in public schools. I believe that all residents should know who is representing them and they should know how to run for office if they aspire to do so.

I know that I am the perfect one to write a book about running for office because I have run two times and I have helped many others run. I have a passion for helping others succeed and I want our communities to be better for us all.

You will enjoy this book. You will learn tips and tricks to run for office and learn how to raise money, so you can reach your campaign goals. This book is not politically charged, however, it discusses the major political ideologies that impact us today.

Now is the time to read this book and run for office. Today's political climate is very perilous and many of the politicians will be either voted out of office or retiring because now is the time to be proactive and not reactive to our issues.

I hope that you enjoy this book and run for office someday. Your service is needed, and it will be greatly appreciated.

# *Author Introduction*

My name is Joshua King and I'm an Army veteran, a Deputy Sheriff, and a union leader. I have spent the last 37 years of my life trying to figure out my place in this world. I believe that everyone was put here for a reason. It took me a long time to figure out what my purpose is and now that I know, my life is very exciting. As we walk down memory lane my purpose will be revealed, and I hope that you all will get to know me a little better.

I was born in Laurel, Mississippi but I was raised in Chesapeake, Virginia. My parents divorced when I was young. I grew up without my father, and my mother worked two jobs to make ends meet. I was the man of the house and I had to take care of my younger brother and sister. However, I did not let my situation deter me.

When I was 16, I wanted to play football but because I was the man of the house, I had to get a job to help my family. I used to walk miles to work in the cold with my apron on and my classmates would drive by me and laugh. However, I didn't let them deter me from my goal. I saved my money and the next spring I drove to work. I bought the latest clothes and shoes and, most importantly, I was supporting my family. No one was laughing at me anymore. Other kids in my community noticed my achievements and this was the beginning of my purpose in life as a community leader.

My brother noticed how good I was doing, and he wanted to be just like me. So, I got him a job with me. Next my friends needed a job, so I got them a job. Finally, those people who were laughing at me, came to me and I got them a job. I had become a community leader and all I was doing was sharing my success.

In 1999, after graduation, I went to community college for two semesters, dropped out and worked odd jobs. Two years later, I joined the Army and found a wife. She became pregnant months later and I was not ready for all the sudden changes in my life.

In 2003, I deployed to Iraq and I was surrounded by death and destruction. I needed to make peace with my situation, so I made a promise to God that if He brought me home safely that I would be a good husband, a good person, and that I would help everyone that I could. Today, that pact still stands, and I know that if I stopped helping others that I would surely die.

While I was in the army I deployed multiple times and unfortunately my young marriage was falling apart. One day my wife notified me that our daughter was diagnosed with autism. I didn't know what autism was and, in my ignorance, I blamed her for the disability. I ended my military service and we divorced shortly after. I was granted custody and I was a single parent for three years until I met my amazing wife, Candi.

During this time, I was recently employed with Fairfax County Sheriff's Office and I needed help with my daughter. I prayed for a good woman and now I'm blessed to have been married for seven years. I got a second chance in life and I wasn't going to waste it.

While employed as a Deputy Sheriff, I volunteered for the Fairfax County Meals on Wheels program and I joined the Fairfax County Deputy Sheriff peer support team. As a team member, I supported fellow coworker veterans by helping them apply for disability compensation and educational benefits. Which resulted in many of them receiving compensation and others continuing their education and graduating.

My wife helped me help others and she encouraged me to go back to school. Subsequently in 2013, I graduated magna cum laude from Northern Virginia Community College. Next, I transferred to George Mason University and my life started to make sense.

And then suddenly, something tragic happened. My 11-year-old daughter went an entire year without a school teacher. Her special needs teacher got her Master's in A.B.A. therapy and when she asked Prince William County Public Schools for more money, they could not compensate her.  She resigned and took a job elsewhere leaving my daughter and six other students without a teacher. The principal had two teacher's aides teach the class for the remainder of the year because they could not fill the position.

The next General Assembly session I went down to Richmond to advocate for my issues. Unfortunately, no legislation was passed to remedy our issues. I grew tired of waiting for our elected officials to resolve our issues, so I ran for the Virginia House of Delegates in 2015 and lost by 125 votes.

I ran again in 2017 and lost in the primary by 12 votes. It was a hard loss for me, but I had to continue serving my community. I helped everyone I could and when Prince William county made history by electing five Democratic Delegates, I felt proud because I was part of the process. During my race, I raised $134,000, graduated from GMU, and I kept my family together. I am truly blessed, and I will continue my service until the next time I run for office.

Today, I spend time with my three children, Josclyn, Candis, and Joshua, Jr. We spend time doing homework, Girl Scouts, and playing board games. I enjoy cooking, writing, playing video games, and watching movies.

Thank you all for going down memory lane with me. Now that I have found my purpose as a community leader, I must replicate my success in others and continue my service as a public servant. Thank you for giving me this opportunity to share my experience with you. I look forward to campaigning with you all one day.

# *Chapter 1*

# Political Ideologies

Choosing to align yourself with a political party is a personal decision. It is a decision that will determine your values and it is the first step in performing your civic duty. In this chapter, we will discuss what political ideologies were formed and the distinct implications that they have. Among these ideologies are liberalism, radicalism, and conservatism. Many thinkers have helped shape these ideologies and most of their views still exist today. Thinkers such as Jeremy Bentham, Karl Marx, and Edmonde Burke will be examined and analyzed for their contributions to the aforementioned ideologies. After reading these ideologies, you will be able to choose which party is consistent with your beliefs. Before you declare whether your Democratic (liberalism), Independent (radicalism), or Republican (conservatism), you will have enough information to make an informed decision. This chapter is important because it will give you an overview of the ideologies that will help you when you choose to run for public office.

**Liberalism** is a philosophy that places a heavy emphasis on freedom, equality, and opportunity. In most cases, it also involves an openness to change and a desire to seek new solutions to problems. It also emphasizes that cooperation can promote peace by diplomacy in international relations. Liberty for liberalists is a freedom from social oppression. They believe that humans are rational and can make the right choices. Equality for them would be equal opportunity, but not economic equality. They support private property and believe that change is gradual/incremental (Minogue, Girvetz, Dagger, & Ball, 2018).

Jeremy Bentham was one of the earliest liberalist who took on social justice issues. He advocated for individual and economic freedom, the separation of church and state, freedom of expression, equal rights for women, the right to divorce, and the decriminalization of homosexual acts. He called for the abolition of slavery, the death penalty, and physical punishment. He also advocated for animal rights and he opposed the idea of natural law and natural rights and called them "nonsense upon stilts." He also believed in a free market and that gender and sex should be equal. He was the founder of modern utilitarianism. In his work, Bentham's *A Fragment on Government*, he notes, "it is the greatest happiness of the greatest number that is the measure of right and wrong" (Duignan & Plamenatz, 2018).

**Radicalism** emphasizes the need to find and eliminate the basic injustices of society. One of the biggest issues is the gap between the wealthy and the poor. They also analyze the root causes of the divide to find a way to bridge the gap. Liberty for radicals is putting economic freedom before political freedom. Their rationality is fueled by passion and reason and economic equality is it a top priority. Traditionally, radicals also disagree with owning private property and they believe in revolution to bring the system down (Karl Marx, 2018).

Karl Marx was a well-known radical for his ideas and his work in his pamphlet the *Communist Manifesto*. Marx's theory holds that human societies develop through class struggle. The conflict was between ruling classes (known as the bourgeoisie) that control the means of production and working classes (known as the proletariat) that work on these means by selling their labor for wages. Marx argued that capitalism facilitated social relations and ideology through commodification, inequality, and the exploitation of labor. He believes that states are run in the interests of the ruling class, but are, nonetheless, represented as being in favor of the common interest of all. He predicted that capitalism produced internal tensions which would lead to its self-destruction and replacement by a new system which he called socialism (Karl Marx, 2018).

**Conservatism** places great emphasis on traditional values, institutions, and ideas. Conservatives are generally distrustful of change, risk, and reform. It focuses on maintaining the status quo and limiting government involvement. Liberty for them is limiting freedom because it creates social chaos. This rational group believes that individuals need guidance and believes that equality should be based on a hierarchy. They are strong supporters of private property and are resistant to change.

Edmonde Burke was a modern conservative of his time. He advocated that individuals must be led by an enlightened leader and that too much freedom is a threat to social order. He believed that humans are ruled by passion rather than reason and he favored a hierarchal based society. In his work the *"Reflections on the French Revolution,"* he famously quoted that:

> "If civil society be made for the advantage of man, all the advantages for which is made become his right...Men have a right to...justice; as between their fellows, whether their fellows are in politic function or in ordinary occupation. They have a right to the fruits of their industry; and to the means of making their industry fruitful. They have a right to the acquisitions of their parents; to

the nourishment and improvement of their offspring; to instruction in life, and to consolation in death. "

He was a strong supporter of private property because it led to order and stability in society. He promoted tradition and continuity over change and was an advocate of a strong military state to keep the balance of power (The Basics of Philosophy, 2018).

In conclusion, liberalism, radicalism and conservatism represent different views for different types of individuals in society. A mix of the ideologies in a state such as the U.S. is needed to help form a perfect union of ideas that represent the populations best interest. States must have some form of social welfare to maintain values and economic order to keep in power. Radicalism has to exist to keep the balance of power between liberalism and conservatism. When one gets out of hand, radicals help maintain peace and stability of the state.

# Chapter 2

# Choosing Your Office

The office that you seek is carefully chosen based on the issues you want to change. If your issues are school related, you might be inclined to run for school board. School board member responsibilities include setting the vision and goals for the district, adopting policies to help set priorities, and managing the collective bargaining process for employees of the district (GreatSchools Staff, 2018).

If your issues are state funding and law making, the House of Representatives, or General Assembly is the office you want to pursue. This body of government consists of 100 members who are elected for two-year terms. The position is part-time, and requires frequent visits to the statehouse for voting and government business (Political Campaign Tips, 2018).

Another powerful position is mayor. Running for Mayor of a city is usually a four-year elected position, however, it can be part-time in smaller cities, towns and townships (Political Campaign Tips, 2018). Mayors' duties include developing and proposing policies. Additionally, they carry out the council's directives by implementing the policies that they adopted (MRSC, 2018).

Whatever office you choose, do the research. You will be most effective if you are in the right office for your issues. Public service is about your constituents. How can you better serve your community is the question you must answer for yourself. Public officials have full time responsibilities that comes with little pay and many of the decisions you will make will either provide relief or harm many. Choose wisely!

# Election cycles

Did you know that in the Commonwealth of Virginia there is an election every year? It can be very confusing because only federal and statewide races are on T.V. and radio due to the high cost. Unfortunately, there are more local races that residents disregard and rarely vote for every year and that results in poor voter turnout and less representation. Many voters don't even know who their elected officials are nor what they do. Below is the actual five-year Virginia election cycle and here is a link to find out some of your elected officials:

***https://whosmy.virginiageneralassembly.gov/.***

| 2015 | 2016 | 2017 | 2018 | 2019 |
|---|---|---|---|---|
| **MAY 5**<br>Town Council (1 town)<br>Vienna (2-year term) | **MAY 3**<br>**City Council** (17 cities)<br>(terms vary - set by Charter)<br>**City School Boards** (10 cities)<br>(terms same as City Council )<br>**Town Council** (114 towns)<br>(terms vary - set by Charter)<br>**City or Town Mayor**<br>**Town Treasurer**<br>**Town Recorder (Clerk)**<br>If required by Charter (terms vary - set by Charter)<br>**Primary** if held: March 1 | **MAY 2**<br>Town Council (1 town)<br>Vienna (2-year term) | **MAY 1**<br>**City Council** (17 cities) (terms vary - set by Charter)<br>**City School Boards** (10 cities)<br>(terms same as City Council )<br>**Town Council** (120 towns)<br>(terms vary - set by Charter)<br>**City or Town Mayor**<br>**Town Treasurer**<br>**Town Recorder (Clerk)**<br>If required by Charter (terms vary - set by Charter)<br>**Primary** if held: March 6 | **MAY 7**<br>Town Council (1 town)<br>Vienna (2-year term) |
| **NOVEMBER 3**<br>**Virginia Senate** (40)<br>(4-year term)<br>**House of Delegates** (100)<br>(2-year term)<br>**Soil and Water Directors**<br>(4-year term)<br>**Counties:**<br>8-year term: *Clerk of Court<br>4-year terms:<br>*Commonwealth's Attorney<br>*Sheriff<br>Commissioner of Revenue<br>*Treasurer<br>Boards of Supervisors (95 counties)<br>School Boards (88 counties)<br>**City Council** (4 cities)<br>(terms vary - set by Charter)<br>**City School Board** (4 cities)<br>(terms vary - set by Charter)<br>**Town Council** (11 Towns)<br>(terms vary – set by Charter)<br>**Primary** if held: June 9 | **NOVEMBER 8**<br>**President**<br>(4-year term)<br>**U. S. Representative** (11)<br>(2-year term)<br>**County Board** (1 county)<br>Arlington (4-year term)<br>**County School Board** (1 county)<br>Arlington (4-year term)<br>**City Council** (17 cities)<br>(terms vary - set by Charter)<br>**City School Board** (9 cities)<br>(terms vary - set by Charter)<br>**Town Council** (54 towns)<br>(terms vary - set by Charter)<br>**Town School Board** (3 towns)<br>(terms vary - set by Charter)<br>**Presidential Primary**<br>(if held: March 1)<br>**Primary - All Other Offices**<br>(if held: June 14) | **NOVEMBER 7**<br>Governor<br>Lieutenant Governor<br>**Attorney General**<br>(4-year term)<br>**House of Delegates** (100)<br>(2-year term)<br>**Cities:**<br>4-year terms:<br>*Commonwealth's Attorney<br>*Sheriff<br>Commissioner of Revenue<br>*Treasurer<br>**Counties:**<br>4-year terms:<br>Boards of Supervisors (58 counties)<br>School Boards (53 counties)<br>**City Council** (3 cities)<br>(terms vary - set by Charter)<br>**City School Board** (4 cities)<br>(terms vary - set by Charter)<br>**Town Council** (12 Towns)<br>(terms vary – set by Charter)<br>**Primary** if held: June 13 | **NOVEMBER 6**<br>**U. S. Senator (1)**<br>(6-year term)<br>**U. S. Representative** (11)<br>(2-year term)<br>**County Board** (1 county)<br>Arlington (4-year term)<br>**County School Board** (1 county)<br>Arlington (4-year term)<br>**City Council** (16 cities) (terms vary - set by Charter)<br>**City School Board** (8 cities)<br>(terms vary - set by Charter)<br>**Town Council** (55 towns)<br>(terms vary - set by Charter)<br>**Town School Board** (2 towns)<br>(terms vary - set by Charter)<br>**Primary** if held: June 12 | **NOVEMBER 5**<br>**Virginia Senate** (40)<br>(4-year term)<br>**House of Delegates** (100)<br>(2-year term)<br>**Soil and Water Directors**<br>(4-year term)<br>**Counties:**<br>8-year term: *Clerk of Court<br>4-year terms:<br>*Commonwealth's Attorney<br>*Sheriff<br>Commissioner of Revenue<br>*Treasurer<br>Boards of Supervisors (95 counties)<br>School Boards (88 counties)<br>**City Council** (4 cities)<br>(terms vary - set by Charter)<br>**City School Board** (4 cities)<br>(terms vary - set by Charter)<br>**Town Council** (11 Towns)<br>(terms vary – set by Charter)<br>**Primary** if held: June 11 |

COMMONWEALTH OF VIRGINIA **SCHEDULE OF GENERAL ELECTIONS** DEPARTMENT OF ELECTIONS

↑ **If a city shares these offices with a county, then the city elects at the same time as the county. REV 02/17/2016**

(Virginia Department of Elections, 2016)

# Chapter 3

# Getting on the Ballot

Now that you have chosen the office that you want to run for, you have to formally declare the office your seeking with the Virginia Department of Elections. As a candidate, you must meet certain qualifications, file the required documents, and pay your filing **fee** in order to appear on the ballot.

## Primary Filing Fee

Primary election candidates are required to pay a filing fee. The fee must be paid prior to filing the Declaration of Candidacy form. The receipt for payment must be submitted with the Declaration. Please note that if compensation for the office sought is paid in whole or in part by fees, the candidate's primary filing fee will be fixed by the committee of your party. Additionally, the filing fee will be $5.00 if no salary or fee is attached to the office sought. All other candidates are required to pay a fee of 2% of the annual salary for the office sought (Virginia Department of Elections, 2018).

## Forms to be Completed

Candidates must be qualified to vote for the office sought and be a Virginia resident for at least one year prior to the election. The candidate bulletin for the office sought should be read and the Certificate of Candidate Qualification Form must be completed. This form can be filed any time after January 1 of the election year. Additional forms such as Campaign Finance documents, a Declaration of Candidacy form, and the appropriate Statement of Economic Interest form must be completed and uploaded to the Department of Elections. Be aware that you must file the forms before the filing deadline or your name will not be on the ballot

(Virginia Department of Elections, 2018).

Another relevant form to get you on the ballot is the Petition of Qualified Voters. This is a two-page document printed on one piece of 8½" x 11" paper. If you are unable to print this form back and front, call 800-552-9745 or 804-864-8901 and a form will be sent to you. All of the signatures do not have to be on the same page of the petition and numerous pages can be circulated by a legal resident of the United States of America. Please note that the circulator cannot be a minor nor a felon whose voting rights have not been restored. The circulator must also swear or affirm that he/she personally witnessed the signature of each voter on the affidavit provided on the petition (Virginia Department of Elections, 2018).

Now that you have printed out the forms, you must get at least 125 signatures to get on the ballot. It is advisable to get at least 300 signatures because each signature must be verified. Signatures may be disqualified if the registered voter incorrectly filled out the form or did not sign it. Residents may have signed it and they are not qualified to vote in the next election because they failed to update their address and other information. A resident can check/update their information at https://www.elections.virginia.gov/voter-outreach/update registration.html (Virginia Department of Elections, 2018). Here are sample forms that must be filed.

CERTIFICATE OF CANDIDATE QUALIFICATION
**LOCAL OFFICES**
**NOTICE:** YOU MUST FILE THIS FORM WITH THE GENERAL REGISTRAR
BY THE FILING DEADLINE. FAILURE TO DO SO MAY RESULT IN
YOUR DISQUALIFICATION. SEE REVERSE SIDE FOR DETAILS.
Pursuant to § 24.2-501 of the *Code of XXXX*, I hereby certify that:
1. I am a citizen of the United States. [ ] YES [ ] NO
2. I am at least eighteen years of age or will be on or before the date of the
election for the office I am seeking.
[ ] YES [ ] NO
3. I have been a resident of the Commonwealth of Virginia for the year
immediately preceding the election for the office I am seeking.
[ ] YES [ ] NO
4. I now reside at the address shown below in the *county or city and, if
applicable, district in which I seek office [residence address must be given; post
office box or general delivery **is not** acceptable]:

_______________________________________________________________
STREET AND NUMBER, RURAL ROUTE AND BOX NUMBER, OR HIGHWAY ROUTE NUMBER
**City/Town** ______________________________________ **ZIP** ___________
**[If town, also list County of residence**: _______________________________ ]
5. I am registered to vote at the above address in the precinct in which I reside.
[or my application for registration, transfer, or change of address is on file in
the general registrar's office]
[ ] YES [ ] NO
6. Have you ever been convicted of a felony or any other crime that would
preclude you  from holding office? (See, e.g., § 18.2-472)
[ ] YES [ ] NO
7. Have you ever been adjudicated mentally incompetent **and** lost your right to
vote? [ ] YES [ ] NO
8. If you answered **YES** to 6, give date of certificate restoring voting rights.
If **YES** to 7, give date of court order restoring competency.
_______________________ **DATE OF RESTORATION**
9. I am an attorney admitted to the bar of the Commonwealth.
(Answer only if seeking office of Commonwealth's Attorney)
[ ] YES [ ] NO

| PLEASE **TYPE** OR **PRINT LEGIBLY** ALL THE FOLLOWING INFORMATION: | OFFICE SOUGHT |
|---|---|
| YOUR NAME AS IT IS TO APPEAR ON BALLOT [SEE **REVERSE SIDE** FOR REQUIREMENTS] | DISTRICT IF APPLICABLE |
| MAILING OR CAMPAIGN ADDRESS | YOUR SOCIAL SECURITY NUMBER [SEE STATEMENT ON **REVERSE SIDE**] |
| ELECTION DATE (MM/DD/YYYY) | |

| CHECK ONE | Republican Primary Special Election<br>Democratic Primary General Election |
|---|---|
| E-MAIL ADDRESS | (AREA CODE) HOME TELEPHONE |
| WEB ADDRESS | (AREA CODE) BUSINESS TELEPHONE |

I do solemnly swear [or affirm] subject to penalty provisions for making false statements that the information given
above is true and correct and that I am qualified to vote for and hold the office for which I am a candidate.

| PLACE PHOTOGRAPHICALLY REPRODUCIBLE NOTARY SEAL/STAMP BELOW | SIGNATURE OF CANDIDATE | DATE |
|---|---|---|

State of County/City of _________________________________
The foregoing instrument was subscribed and sworn before me this day of
, 20 , by ___________________________________________ .
PRINT NAME OF CANDIDATE

| | |
|---|---|
| _____________________________ <br> SIGNATURE OF NOTARY OR CLERK OF CIRCUIT COURT | ___________________ <br> ___________________ |
| NOTARY REGISTRATION NUMBER | DATE NOTARY COMMISSION EXPIRES |

**KNOWINGLY MAKING ANY UNTRUE STATEMENT OR ENTRY IN THIS DOCUMENT IS A FELONY UNDER VIRGINIA LAW.**
**THE PUNISHMENT IS A MAXIMUM FINE OF $2,500 AND/OR CONFINEMENT FOR UP TO TEN YEARS.**
**ALSO, YOU LOSE YOUR RIGHT TO VOTE.**
*See §15.2-1525 of the *Code of Virginia* for certain exceptions to residence requirements for
Commonwealth's Attorneys.
SBE-501(4) REV 7/18 SEE **INSTRUCTIONS ON REVERSE SIDE**
(Virginia Department of Elections, 2018)

**CONTINUED FROM REVERSE SIDE CANDIDATE NAME:** __________________ **OFFICE SOUGHT:** ________________________

| |
|---|
| **CIRCULATOR:** MUST SWEAR OR AFFIRM IN THE AFFIDAVIT BELOW THAT S/HE IS A LEGAL RESIDENT OF THE UNITED STATES OF AMERICA, NOT A MINOR NOR A FELON WHOSE VOTING RIGHTS HAVE NOT BEEN RESTORED AND THAT S/HE PERSONALLY WITNESSED EACH SIGNATURE.<br>**SIGNER:** YOUR SIGNATURE ON THIS PETITION MUST BE YOUR OWN AND DOES NOT SIGNIFY AN INTENT TO VOTE FOR THE CANDIDATE. YOU MAY SIGN PETITIONS FOR MORE THAN ONE CANDIDATE. |

| OFFICE USE ONLY ▼ | SIGNATURE OF REGISTERED VOTER [PRINT NAME IN SPACE BELOW SIGNATURE] | POST OFFICE BOXES ARE NOT ACCEPTABLE RESIDENCE ADDRESS House Number and Street Name **or** Rural Route and Box Number and City/Town | DATE SIGNED [Must be after January 1 of election year] | *SEE NOTE BELOW LAST 4 DIGITS OF SOCIAL SECURITY NUMBER [OPTIONAL] |
|---|---|---|---|---|
| | SIGN | RESIDENCE | | |
| PRINT | CITY/TOWN | | | |
| 8. | SIGN | RESIDENCE | | |
| PRINT | CITY/TOWN | | | |
| | SIGN | RESIDENCE | | |
| PRINT | CITY/TOWN | | | |
| 10. | SIGN | RESIDENCE | | |
| PRINT | CITY/TOWN | | | |
| | SIGN | RESIDENCE | | |
| PRINT | CITY/TOWN | | | |
| 12. | SIGN | RESIDENCE | | |
| PRINT | CITY/TOWN | | | |
| *Commonwealth of Virginia* **- AFFIDAVIT -** | | | | |

I,

_______________________________, swear or affirm that (i) my full residential address is

_______________________________ in the State/Commonwealth of

_______________________________; in the County/City/Town of

_______________________________;

(ii) I am a legal resident of the United States of America; (iii) I am not a minor; (iv) I am not a felon whose voting rights have not been restored; and (v) I witnessed the signature of each person who signed this page or its reverse side. I understand that falsely signing this affidavit is a felony punishable by a maximum fine up to $2,500 and/or imprisonment up to ten years.

_______________________________

PLACE PHOTOGRAPHICALLY REPRODUCIBLE SIGNATURE OF PERSON CIRCULATING THE PETITION NOTARY SEAL/STAMP BELOW DATE
State of _______________________________
County/City of _______________________________
The foregoing instrument was subscribed and sworn before me this
_______ day of
_______________________________, 20 _____,
by

_______________________________

_______________________________.

CIRCULATOR'S DRIVER'S LICENSE NUMBER, IF APPLICABLE

| | | | | |
|---|---|---|---|---|
| PRINT NAME OF PERSON CIRCULATING THE PETITION<br><br>______________________________<br><br>______________________________<br><br>SIGNATURE OF NOTARY OR OTHER PERSON AUTHORIZED TO ADMINISTER OATHS NOTARY REGISTRATION NUMBER** DATE NOTARY COMMISSION EXPIRES** | | | | |
| NAME OF STATE THAT ISSUED THE CIRCULATOR'S DRIVER'S LICENSE | | | | |
| CIRCULATOR'S LAST 4 DIGITS OF SOCIAL SECURITY NUMBER | | | | |
| *** Privacy notice**: The Code of XXXX, §§ 24.2-506 and 24.2-521, authorizes requesting the last four digits of your social security number to facilitate<br>checking this petition with the official voter registration record. You are not required to provide this information and may sign the petition without<br>doing so. The State Board of Elections or the General Registrar, when copying this document for public inspection, must cover the column containing<br>any social security number or part thereof.<br>** If not included in seal/stamp. SBE-506/521 REV 1.2013 | | | | |

(Virginia Department of Elections, 2018)

## Further Instructions

Read Local Candidate Bulletin:

https://www.elections.virginia.gov/Files/BecomingACandidate/CandidateBulletins/2018-11-06%20Gen%20and%20Sp%20Bulletin%20Local%20and%20Constitutional%20rev%2003-02-18.pdf

Follow Steps:

1.  File for EIN

https://sa.www4.irs.gov/modiein/individual/index.jsp

You are exempt from filing an 8871 for local office

2.  Get a P.O. Box

Make sure the name of the 'company' opening the box matched what your Campaign Committee will be named.

https://www.usps.com/manage/po-boxes.htm

3.  Declaration of Candidacy

https://www.elections.virginia.gov/Files/Forms/Candidates/SBE_505_520_Declaration_of_Candidacy_Rev1_15.pdf

4.  Statement of Organization

https://www.elections.virginia.gov/Files/Forms/Candidates/StatementOrganizationCandidate.pdf

Pick Treasurer

Include Bank Account Info - The bank name and city where you will be opening an account

Setup/File this online:
https://cf.elections.virginia.gov/Account/LogOn?ReturnUrl=%2f

5.  Open a Bank Account

Bring your printed-out SOO & EIN

Tell the bank teller that you are a 527 Political non-profit and you are unincorporated

You want a Community Checking Account

6.  Certificate of Candidate Qualifications

Certificate of Candidate Qualification – Local Offices

7.  Statement of Economic Interest

https://www.elections.virginia.gov/Files/BecomingACandidate/2017-StateandLocalSOEI.pdf

8.  Certified Petitions

https://www.elections.virginia.gov/Files/Forms/Candidates/Petition-of-Qualified-Voters-SBE-506_521_letter.pdf

9.  Primary Filing Fee

(For partisan races) Check with local Democratic Committee about your filing fee

# *Chapter 4*

# Developing Your Message

In this chapter you will examine yourself and start developing your message. Your message is specific and unique to you. As we explore my message (aka stump speech), you will be able to craft your message. Your stump will be the bread and butter of your campaign. An effective stump will not only get you votes, but it will get you the money needed to run a successful campaign.

First, you have to decide who your target audience is and once that is decided, you need to figure out what you have to say to persuade them to volunteer, vote, and donate to you. There are two stump speeches that you must master. The first is your three to six minute speech which is used for meet and greets, churches and larger campaign events. The second stump speech is your 30-60 second speech that you will use at doors when you talk to voters and with people you meet as you go out in the field.

**Characteristics of good messages have many different elements which are equally important.**

- **Short and direct.** Voters time is precious and they have very little patience for listening to long-winded politicians. You must effectively deliver your message in 60 seconds or less. If you cannot, then you will lose their attention and probably their vote (Brian O'Day, 2018).

- **Truthfullness and Crediblilty**. The message should come from a candidates values, practices and background (Brian O'Day, 2018). A good example of this is when a veteran goes in a room full of veterans and talks about veteran issues. Veterans value other veterans and if you are not a veteran and pretend to know, you will be called out and lose all credibility.

- **Persuasiveness and Importance**. You must talk about challenges the voters face everyday. These issues must be important to your target audience. Voters are more likely to support a candidate who can speak to their issues. Always remember that you are trying to convince the voter that you are the best candidate to represent them (Brian O'Day, 2018).

- **Show Contrast.** Voters will make a choice between you and other candidates and you need to make it clear how you are different from the other candidates. (Brian O'Day, 2018). If your opponent is pro- choice, then you tell them your pro-life. If you are for legalizing maraijuana and raising the minimun wage, be vocal about how you are different and let voters know that you are the one to get it done.

A question you will hear daily is why are you running for office? In order to answer this question, you should make a list of all the reasons why voters should vote for you. Next, choose the most compelling reason and write a brief statement and read it aloud to yourself. This statement should be a minute or less. If it is too long, you must trim it and check the message to make sure that it is credible and truthful (Brian O'Day, 2018). You will need this part of your speech for your next assignment.

An example of my three to six minute stump speech is as follows:

Good Evening, my name is Josh King and I'm an Army Veteran, a Deputy Sheriff, and a community leader, and I'm running to be your next Delegate for the 2<sup>nd</sup> House District which covers Woodbridge and Stafford.

I am running because our schools are overcrowded and our children can't get a world class education because their teachers are overworked and underpaid. I know this for sure because I have an 11-year-old daughter who has autism who went an entire year without a teacher.

Last school year, my daughter's teacher obtained her Master's Degree and when she went back to ask for more money, they could not afford to pay her more. She left the county leaving seven autistic children with two teacher's aides to teach them for the year. It is unacceptable for any student to have to go a year without a teacher because the state does not provide enough support to retain teachers in our county. I'm running to make sure that no child, especially a child with special needs goes an entire year without a school teacher.

My next issue is mass transportation. The express lanes are not the answer. There is no transparency on the prices and they do not relieve traffic congestion. We no longer live in a rural area. Woodbridge and Stafford are growing faster than our transportation system can expand. We need to look for long-term solutions that will increase our quality of life and reduce our traffic congestion.

Finally, we need more quality jobs in our district. We have Quantico to the south, DC to the north and Fort Belvoir in the middle. Most of my neighbors are federal employees, government contractors, or military. We need to decentralize Northern Virginia and bring jobs to our district. We have a talented work force and better schools and commute times will help attract businesses and their employees to the area.

We live in a great area, but it can be even better if we pull together and support each other. I ask three things of you all. First, I ask for your time. You can volunteer by knocking on doors, phone banking, or hosting meet and greets. Next, I need you to donate to my campaign. In order to run an effective race, we need money to get the word out. Lastly, I need your vote. We can do nothing if we don't have a seat at the table. Thank you all for your support and I look forward to serving as your delegate!

## Developing your stump

Now that you have read my speech, lets break it down and develop your speech as we go through mine.

**Introduction**. Good evening, my name is Josh King and I am an Army Veteran, a Deputy Sheriff, and a community leader, and I am running to be your next Delegate for the $2^{nd}$ House District which covers Woodbridge and Stafford.

Here, you tell your audience your name and what you do (Coach, Writer, Activist, Teacher). Please use at least three. Then, you tell them what office you are running for and where it is.

Good evening, my name is (blank) and I am a (blank), (blank), (blank) and I am running to be your next (blank).

**Why are you running?** I am running because our schools are overcrowded and our children can't get a world class education because their teachers are overworked and underpaid. I know this for sure because I have an 11-year old-daughter who has autism who went an entire year without a teacher.

I am running because (blank) and (blank). Add compelling personal story.

**Compelling personal story-** Last school year, my daughter's teacher obtained her Master's Degree and when she went back to ask for more money, they could not afford to pay her more. She left the county leaving seven autistic children with two teacher's aides to teach them for the year. It is unacceptable for any student to have to go a year without a teacher because the state does not provide enough support to retain teachers in our county. I'm running to make sure that no child, especially a child with special needs goes an entire year without a school teacher.

Tell your story with at least three-six issues (mental health, childcare, taxes, transportation, womens rights).

The **Ask-** We live in a great area, but it can be even better if we pull together and support each other. I ask three things of you all. First, I ask for your time. You can volunteer by knocking on doors, phone banking, or hosting meet and greets. Next, I need you to donate to my campaign. In order to run an effective race, we need money to get the word out.

Lastly, I need your vote. We can do nothing if we don't have a seat at the table. Thank you all for your support and I look forward to serving as your delegate!

The **ask** is one of the most important elements of your speech. Voters are looking for leadership. Have a clear direct ask for your constituents. Never leave without asking for something!

What is your ask? (donation, phone banking, letter stuffing, door knocking)

Write the speech and say it out loud. Record yourself and listen to it as you go to work. Have different versions of your stump speech and always know your audience.

## Trimming your Stump

Next, we will transform my three to six minute speech into a 30/60 second stump speech.

**30 seconds-** Good evening, my name is Josh King and I am an Army Veteran, a Deputy Sheriff, and a community leader, and I am running to be your next Delegate for the 2nd House District which covers Woodbridge and Stafford.

I am running because my autistic daughter went an entire year without a teacher because her teacher was overworked and underpaid.

My issues are education, transportation, economic development, womens rights and the enviroment.

I believe that we live in a great area, but it can be even better if we pull together and support each other. I ask three things. I need your time, financial support, and your vote. Thank you for giving me this opportunity.

**60 seconds-** Good evening, my name is Josh King and I'm an Army Veteran, a Deputy Sheriff, and a community leader, and I'm running to be your next Delegate for the 2nd House District which covers Woodbridge and Stafford.

I'm running because our schools are overcrowded and our children can't get a world class education because their teachers are overworked and underpaid. I know this for sure because I have an 11-year-old daughter who has autism who went an entire year without a teacher.

***(Add compelling story)***- Last school year, my daughter's teacher obtained her Master's Degree and when she went back to ask for more money, they could not afford to pay her more. She left the county leaving seven autistic children with two teacher's aides to teach them for the year. It is unacceptable for any student to have to go a year without a teacher because the state does not provide enough support to retain teachers in our county.

My issues are education, transportation, economic development, womens rights and the enviroment.

I believe that we live in a great area, but it can be even better if we pull together and support each other. I ask three things. I need your time, your support, and your vote. Thank you for giving me this opportunity.

Once you have completed your three to six minute speech, all you have to do is trim it down and hit the highlights.

# Chapter 5

# Identifying Your Base

**What is a Base?** This term **base** refers to targeted voters and groups who support you because you are affliated with them through party, religion, race, gender identity, or sexual preference. These voters may support you because you're from the business community or you might be part of a union. Your base will vote for you no matter what because they have a vested interest in the outcome of your election.

According to the study by Pew research, the Democratic voters have grown to be more college-educated, younger, more liberal and less religious. The study asserted that Republicans are less likely to be college graduates and that Democrats have benefited from the movement of women and college graduates. Moreover, minority voters of all educational levels mostly side with Democrats which accounts for 40% of Democratic voters and 14% of Republican voters. As recently as two years ago, White college graduates sided with the Democrats 53%-42%. On the other hand, Republicans have increased loyalty among white voters without a college degree who live in rural areas (Lauter, 2018).

## Neglected Bases

In America, residents of color are lumped together into categories and they are underrepresented due to the lack of care of individual subsets having their own issues. African Americans and Hispanics are among these groups and their issues are often left out. However, the Democratic party heavily relies on minorities to vote for them. An example of a subgroup who's issues are underrepresentated are Africans, not African Amercans. Africans have different but similar issues than African Americans. While Blacks all suffer from petty traffic stops by police, police shootings and the like, Africans have immigration challenges.

Many African immigrants are very educated and are not descendants from slaves and yet they are lumped into African-American subgroups. Not all Hispanics have the same issues. Some hispanics get harassed about their immigration status and many do not have adequate legal representation to assist them through the court system. Their issues have been neglected and ignored for years. People of color shaped the U.S. and now it is time for the government to represent minorities in a proactive manor.

In an effort to motivate more minorities to vote the in the 2018 midterms, the Democratic National Committee (DNC) is targeting minority voters again. In the New York Times article, *Democrats Plan New Effort to Target Minority Voters*, columnist Astead W. Herndon noted that the DNC plans to split $1.2 million across 16 state parties to hire community organizers to target Black, Latino, Asian, millennial and rural voters. The plan will introduce a new database that could potentially identify 25 million new Democratic voters who are currently unregistered (Herndon, 2018). The problem is not that these groups won't vote, the problem is that when they vote they are not represented by those they elect and their issues have never been resolved. Remember that your base is your lifeline and those you wish to serve are those you do not forget once you get into office.

## Determining Your Base

When determining which groups will be your base, you have to look at the groups, clubs, professional organizations and political ideologies you belong to. I'm a 37-year-old, college educated, veteran who is married with children. My target groups are going to be young people between the ages of 26 and 45, small business owners, and parents with school-age children (Brian O'Day, 2018). My base also includes veterans, law enforcement, teachers, parents with children with special needs, and labor unions. Your base could be churches, women's rights groups, environmentalists, property owners or nurses. Your office, your background and your message will determine who you should target to be in your base.

An important part of defining your base is determining which demographic groups will not be part of your targeted audience. You should, for example, state explicitly "we will not take dirty money," which means you won't take money from coal companies or businesses that pollute the environment. It is important to know which demographic groups you are willing to give to your opponents once you have decided which groups are yours. For example, pro-gun owners and law enforcement supporters are going to have the least in common with groups like Black Lives Matter. If you have targeted one group, you will most likely give the other group to your opponents (Brian O'Day, 2018).

# Chapter 6
# Local Parties

Local parties are the backbones of every community. The local party moves mountains for the residents they serve and the candidates they help elect. Every community has locally elected public officials and the local party is where many of them go for support and ideas to better serve their communities. This chapter will discuss how your local party can help you get elected. You will learn how to build your campaign team and what roles and responsiblilties they have.

Joining your local party is the first step. Most parties have a website that can be found with a simple internet search. Some parties meet once a month and many parties have subcommittees that meet once a month. For example, subcommittees range from gay rights, disabilities, criminal justice and urban development to guns, public safety, and zoning. When you join your local party, see which committees they have available and if they don't have a certain committee, you can start one. These committees can give you valuable insight on local challenges that your constituents face.

Now that you have joined your local party, it is time to get to work. Once you have decided which office you want to run for and why, your next step is to talk to your local party chair. When you meet with the chair you must be ready to answer the question, why you are running. Ask for advise and mentorship. The party chair or designee will give you the information needed to run for the office you seek. You will get information on forms that need to be filed and important deadlines you must meet to get on the ballot. As you attend monthly meetings, you will meet other party members who you will ask to help you on your race.

Politics is all about relationships. You must build a rapport with others to make a team of individuals who will support you throughout your race.

## Building a Campaign Team

Your local party has now been notified that you are interested in running for office. It's time to build your team. Your team will consist of a finance director, campaign manager, field director, mail firm and volunteers. Each member of your team is vital to your success. The positions listed above are the bare minimum needed for your team to be successful. The question is what do they do and how do you find them?

Your local party can provide you with a list of resumes for each position needed. Most local parties have a list of volunteers that always come out to help candidates get elected. Because elections happen every year, there is a constant pool of potential members who will fill these roles. These roles are paid positions so the first position that needs to be filled is the finance director.

## Roles and Responsiblities

The **finance director**'s role is to raise money while working with the candidate, campaign manager, and a finance committee to meet the financial goals of the campaign. They keep the candidate on track, coordinate call time, and oversee all fundraising events (Wellstone, 2018).

The **campaign manager** oversees all aspects of the campaign including day-to-day operations. They manage the staff, create the budget, and coordinate the fundraising operations (Wellstone, 2018). A campaign manager is a direct reflection of the candidate. When you choose someone, make sure that he/she shares your values and ideals. They will often speak in your stead if you can not attend an event.

The **field director**'s main job is to get the message out through direct voter contact. They are responsible for developing a comprehensive plan with volunteers that includes door knocking, phone banking, voter registration and get-out-the vote efforts (Wellstone, 2018).

The **mail firm**'s role is to help you determine your message, logo, walkcards, and mailers. The firm will keep your message consistant with your mailers. Some mail firms have a digital component for ads and commercials. Interview at least three different firms before choosing to make sure that they are a good fit.

A **treasurer** duties includes general financial oversight on present budgets, accounts and financial statements. The treasurer should be on your bank account and he/she will be listed on your statement of organization.

**Volunteers** are the heartbeat of a campaign. They will carry out your many daily tasks such as phone banking, door knocking, and outreach. You must take care of them. Always have some snacks and drinks for them. Please show them some love and they will fight for you until the end and beyond.

Getting your team together is a crucial step toward running for office. Ask your local chair and subcommittees a lot of questions about these positions.  Choose your team carefully and get to work!

# Chapter 7
# Fundraising

Almost everything you do in the campaign will cost something and your finance director should develop an overall budget for the entire campaign. Your budget should not be a wish list, it should be a vital list of items needed to implement your campaign plan. This chapter will discuss how to prepare for fundraising, donors, candidates donor research, call time, endorsements, and fundraising events.

| Item | Cost |
| --- | --- |
| **Direct mail (6 flights)** | **$30,000** |
| Digital ads | $10,000 |
| **Walk lit** | **$7,000** |
| Yard signs | $1,000 |
| **Fundraising** | **$1,000** |
| Staff | TBD |
| **Office Supplies/Miscellaneous** | **$1,000** |
| General Election carryover | $5,000 |
| *Total* | *$55,000 + staff* |

The budget should be the only tool for tracking expenditures, providing goals for fundraisers, and keeping your campaign on track. The budget should be organized week-by-week in order to anticipate what amounts you will need at what time. Have at least three different budgets plans (high, medium, and low) in case your fundraising does not go as planned. The majority of your cost will be on voter contact activities such as printed materials, and door-to-door workers. This cost will account for 70% to 80% of your budget. Administrative costs should be no more than 20% of your total budget. This cost includes office machines, supplies, office staff, and phones (Brian O'Day, 2018). Illustrated is a sample overall primary budget from one of my campaigns.

## Preparing for Fundraising

Setting up a business bank account is required to raise money. Make sure you filed all the required financial paperwork and obtain your FEIN number. Locate a bank that you don't bank with and setup your account. Make sure that your treasurer and finance director are on that account. Order business checks and get a payroll system.

Next, sign up for an Actblue account. Actblue is a secure way to donate, collect, and organize your funds online. They take credit card security seriously and have yearly audits to ensure that they are maintaining a high level of security (Actblue, 2018). Link the Actblue account to a Post Office box. Money contributed through Actblue is collected and distributed weekly to your P.O. Box. Be aware that Actblue takes a small percentage of the funds as a service fee. It is advised that any contribution greater than $250 be mailed or picked up to save on service fees.

## Donors

Before you start raising money, you should make a list of potential donors. Now that you have your message, stump speech and target audience, you can start making your list of people in your inner circle. These people are your friends and family. They will give to you because they love and support you no matter what. Call your network and raise at least 800 dollars to start. You will need the start-up money for access to the Voter Activation Network (VAN). Next, go into your cell phone and check all of your contacts to establish which contacts are personal and which are professional. After you identify who is what, get your finance director to look up their donor histories on VAN.

The advantages of using VAN for fundraising are numerous. Their library of call sheets provides information you will need to make "the ask." Additionally, VAN has easy contribution source tracking that allow the user to know where the money is coming from using hierarchical source codes to help you keep track of it. VAN also uses contact codes that make tagging and searching for donors, prospects and Political Action Committees (PAC) easier using hierarchical codes (NGP VAN, 2018).

## Candidate Donor Research

Gain valuable information about your election by looking at information from past elections. Find out who ran for this position and note past elections and the results. Look at voter turnout and how many votes were needed to win (Brian O'Day, 2018). This information is on Virginia Public Access Project (VPAP).

VPAP is a nonprofit that connects Virginians to nonpartisan information about Virginia politics. The founders believe that it is imperative that citizens have easy access to public documents related to money in politics. Information obtained for VPAP comes directly from public documents such as campaign finance reports, election returns, conflict disclosures, and lobbyist registrations (VPAP, 2018).

The image to the right is based on my campaigns (VPAP, 2018). You can look up any past candidate, review their donors, and set up your budget around those numbers for your race. The donor lists comes from campaign finance reports that must be filed every quarter. When you look up your opponent, you can determine which groups and organizations you should contact for a

# Top Donors

**All Campaigns 2015-2017**

**$78,861** Democratic Party of Virginia

**$69,742** SEIU Committee on Political Education

**$22,901** House Democratic Caucus

**$9,298** Prince William Federation of Teachers

**$8,278** Service Employees International Union - Local 32BJ

**$8,001** Service Employees International Union - Local 512

**$8,000** Service Employees International - 1199

**$7,000** Schaufeld, Karen

**$6,000** United Food & Commercial Workers

**$4,100** Democrats for Route 1 Progress PAC

donation and which ones that you should not contact. As you look at the image, you see that labor unions donated to my campaign. My opponent did not receive an endorsement from these unions and he got endorsements from anti-labor organizations.

Candidate donor research is the fastest way to get all the information needed to run an effective campaign. Go back several years for incumbent races and try to earn their endorsements. My opponent earned the realtor endorsement in my first campaign and that would have been a priority for my next campaign. We will discuss how to obtain an endorsement in the next section.

## Endorsements

As a candidate, you will meet with various group leaders to persuade them to support the campaign. These leaders can be newspaper editorial boards or community-based organizations. A lot of time is spent winning this support early in the campaign when voters aren't paying attention to the election (Brian O'Day, 2018).

Obtaining an endorsement, in most cases, requires a candidate to fill out a candidate questionaire form. After the questionaire is complete, the candidate will mail it back and setup an interview. The interview will be by a panel who will quiz you on your answers on the questionaire. Your campaign team will help you fill out the questionaire. However, you must be very familiar with the questions, answers, the organization core issues and your campaign plan. The questions will be used to determine if you are worthy of the endorsement.

All endorsements are not equal. Most of the endorsements come with financial support and volunteers, but not all of them. Some endorsements aren't worth the time it takes to fill out the questionaire. Be careful of how you spend your time. Before you decide to fill out an endorsement form, do the research on the organization. Carefully research the organization's donor history and past performance before you make a determination if it is worth your time.

# Call Time

Raising money and gaining support is a candidates' main responsibility. It is often referred to as "doors and donors." In this section we will discuss call time. **Call time** is simply the daily grind of calling donors to ask for money. Your stump speech will be slightly modified to persuade donors to give you money. Now that you have gained access to the VAN and you have made your list, it's time to raise money. This is a skill that requires time and patience to perfect. Below is an example of a donor script.

> Hi, may I speak to ____________
>
> This is Josh King, I'm the Secretary of my local SEIU union and the Democratic candidate for House District 2 which is in Woodbridge and northern Stafford counties. How are you?
>
> I wanted to call because the Republican incumbent for this district announced that he's not running for reelection which means that there's now an open seat in a district that both Clinton AND Obama won by 20 points.
>
> I ran for this seat in 2015 and came within 125 votes of beating Delegate Dudenhefer. And now with the Governor's race driving turnout and Dudenhefer retiring, this district is the best chance for Democrats to take a seat back from Republicans in 2017. Can you help put us ahead early by donating $____?

After you receive a contribution, it is advised that you send a thank you letter. An example of a thank you letter is below.

PL XXXX

9512 E HI'll Dr.

Lorton, VA 22079


Dear Paula,


Thank you for your contribution of $25 to my campaign for the House of Delegates. There is no way I would be able to win this race without support from folks like you.

My path to the House of Delegates began thirteen years ago while I was a soldier in the U.S. Army. During my second tour in Iraq, I learned that my daughter, Josclyn, was diagnosed with autism, so I put my Army career on hold so I could return home. When I came home, I not only wanted to be the father she needed, but I also wanted to help other families with autistic children.

Since then I began volunteering to help my fellow veterans reintegrate back into society. While helping them navigate the Veterans Administration, I learned even more about what actually happens in this state. While going to school on the GI Bill and serving as a Deputy Sheriff, I learned more and more about how our education system works and what needs to happen to help veterans access the entitlements and benefits that they have earned.

I've learned that District 2 needs a delegate who will get things done. That's why I promise to focus on the important issues. I'll support our teachers so that all our children can get a world class education. I'll work to create jobs closer to where we live to reduce traffic congestion and increase our quality of life.

You know that I can't do any of these things without first earning our community's trust and support. That's why I so appreciate your faith in me.

Thank you,

Josh King

Candidate for House of Delegates, HD-02

**Call time** can also be used for asking for votes and support during GOTV. An example script is below.

Hi, may I speak to _______?

My name is _______ and I'm a volunteer with Josh King, he's a Democrat from Woodbridge running for the House of Delegates.

Have you decided who you're supporting for Delegate this year?

IF UNDECIDED: I support Josh because I trust him to get things done in Richmond.

Josh is an Army vet and a Deputy Sheriff. He is running because his special needs daughter went a year without a teacher and he wants to make sure every child in the Commonwealth gets a world class education. His other top issues are reducing traffic congestion and creating good paying jobs.

Do you have issues that are important to you?

IF SUPPORTING: Great, thank you! What's your email? We'll be in contact about events and how to get involved with the campaign.

IF AGAINST JOSH: "Okay, thank you. Have a nice day." [End conversation]

**Call time** is the number one way to raise money for your campaign. If done properly, you will raise money with ease. When you call a donor, they know why you are calling. They get hundreds of calls everyday. When you pick up the phone, your 60 seconds starts. Always remember that when someone says no, they might be waiting for you to wow them. Don't give up and keep calling until you get a hard no or an affirmative with money in hand.

## Fundraising Events

Events are a great source of income for your campaign. You can raise money and your name indentity. A successful event is an event where you make more money at the event than you would have made during call time. An event will have at least one host and the host will promise to give or raise an agreed upon amount. Below is an example of an event and a contribution form that is required when you accept money.

# Milton Bratton

*Invites you to a fundraiser in support of*

Josh King

Candidate for VA House of Delegates, District 2

Where: The home of Milton Bratton

37 Bloomington Lane

Stafford, VA 22554

When: Saturday, March 25, 2017

from 3:00 PM to 5:00 PM

RSVP and contribute directly to the event's fundraising page:

https://secure.actblue.com/contribute/page/bratton

Suggested donation levels

$25 Volunteer | $50 Friend | $100 Champion | $250 Host

House of Delegates District 2, which encompasses portions of Prince William and Stafford counties, is a prime target for flipping from red to blue in 2017. President Obama won the district by 18% in 2012, Governor McAuliffe won by 11%, Senator Warner won by 6% in 2014, and Hillary won it by 20%. Josh King lost by only 1% to the Republican incumbent in the last election cycle, but the incumbent announced he will retire this year, making this an open seat.

*Logistical and other questions can be directed to Josh King's Finance Director.*

*Sam Rivers, 301-254-XXXX or sam@kingfordelegate.com*

# King for Delegate Contribution Form

Thank you for supporting our campaign. Please make checks payable to "King for Delegate" or provide your credit card information below. This form can be returned to:

King for Delegate

PO Box 5348, Woodbridge, VA 22194

I am contributing:

By Check __ In Cash __ By Credit Card__ Via Money order__

Amount:

_______________________________________________________________

____________

Credit Card Authorization, if applicable:

Card number ___________________________________________

Exp. Date _______________

Cardholder's signature ________________________________

State law requires us to use our best efforts to collect and report the name, mailing address, and occupation of individuals whose contributions exceed $100 in an election cycle. By donating, you certify that you are a U.S. resident, Green Card holder, or entity registered in the U.S., at least 18 years old, and that this contribution is made from your own funds or the funds of an authorizing corporation or other entity, and that the funds are not being provided by any other person or entity. Check box: ☐

Name of Person (First and Last), Company, or Entity ___________

_______________________

Best phone _______________________________ Phone Type: Work Mobile Home

Email _________________________________________________

Address _______________________________________________

City ___________________________ State _______________

Zip _______________

Occupation (Individuals) ________________________________

Employer or Business's Address __________________________

Employer City ___________________________ Employer State ______

Employer Zip __________

Principal Type of Business (Businesses) ___________________________

# Chapter 8

# Making It Happen

Now that your preparation is complete, it's time to put everything together and get to work. This chapter will cover your daily schedule, deadlines, events, and strategy. Running a campaign is a jog, not a sprint. Every day counts and you will be exhausted. The daily grind is real, however, you will have made it to the end of your race and you will be rewarded for your effort.

On January 1, a candidate can start getting signatures on the petition of qualified voters. You can also file the certificate of candidate qualifications and the statement of economic interests with the local general registrar. The declaration, petitions, and primary filing fee receipt must be submitted by March 29 for your name to appear on the June Primary ballot if applicable (Virginia Department of Elections, 2018).

Within the first three weeks of January you should be interviewing at least three campaign finance directors for a start date of the first week of February. After your selection is complete, your next step is to set weekly fundraising goals and start call time.

The finance director can start coordinating your first event, the campaign kickoff fundraiser. You should invite everyone in your base to this event to include locally-elected officials and your local party. Practice your stump speech and be confident! Make sure to leave some time for other officials to speak during your event.

By the end of March, all of your forms should have been submitted. Continue to raise money, purchase access to the VAN, and start interviewing for additional key members of your team. Always schedule interview times around call-time. Your next hires are your campaign manager, field director, and a mail firm.

## Turf

The field director will start *"cutting your turf"*, which will be used to identify registered voters that you will talk to. Cutting your turf means that the field director will log into the VAN and organize a list of voters in your district. The list (turf) will include information such as a voter's name, address, party affiliation, and phone number. The list will be printed and a walk pack will be created. A walk pack will include a clipboard, turf, a pen and some campaign literature if you have some available. All the voter contacts that you had will be notated in the VAN by your field director. There is also a free app called the Mini VAN that allows the user to digitally access the turf and sync the results.

## Phone Banking

The turf will also be used for *phone banking*. Phone banking is simply calling voters and asking them to vote, volunteer, or attend an event. Some volunteers may not be able to knock on doors but may be willing to make calls on your behalf. Virtual phone banking is optional and allows volunteers to call from home.

## Mail

Once your mail firm has been hired, you can start your photo shoot and get your website up if you haven't already done so. Your website should have your key issues, a volunteer signup form, and a donate button. You should promote your website, events, and information through social media. The mail firm can help set up a Twitter account and a political Facebook account. Be sure to setup a LinkedIn account and have all your links listed.

The mail firm will work with your campaign manager to setup a mail plan. Your mail plan will consist of walk cards and mailers.  You will discuss how many mailers you will use and you will create your logo. Your logo is your trademark. It will help you create name identification. No one knows who you are or what you look like until they have met you personally or receive a piece a literature in the mail or on their door. It takes at least five separate contacts to get a voter to vote once. If you talk to a voter twice in person and send three pieces of mail to them, you made five contacts. Mailers cost anywhere from $3000 to $5000 per piece. I purchased 17 pieces in my general election in 2015 and eight in my 2017 primary. The number of mailers you will use is based on how much money you raise and how many pieces your opponent has sent out.

Mail is your primary means to communicate over a wide area. Your plan will have a mail schedule that will start within your last weeks of your race. Mail will drop twice a week for a general election and once a week for a primary. In addition to mail, a digital component can be added to supplement your mail plan. Digital ads can be boosted on sites like Facebook. Banner ads can be purchased on various political sites like http://bluevirginia.us/. Pre-roll ads can also be purchased on YouTube for a nominal fee.

# Events

Events are a fantastic way to raise money, build name I.D., and find volunteers, donors and voters. Events happen every day somewhere, and you must be very cautious with your time. Never give up call time for an event that is not going to produce you votes or money, especially if the event is not in your district. Most events cost money and if someone invites you to their event, make sure that your ticket is covered by them. Events that you pay for must meet this criterion or you're just wasting time.

Additionally, while at an event, you must make the best use of your time. Introduce yourself to everyone and ask for their business card. Be prepared to say your 30-60 seconds stump speech numerous times. When you receive their card, write a special note about them on the back. Take a variety of photos with all the elected officials and attendees. Most events are two hours long and the speakers usually speak at the top of the hour. Ask the host if you can have three minutes to address the crowd and make your ask. Never leave an event empty handed.

## Sample Deadlines Chart

The chart below is an example of deadlines that you must adhere to file for office, get on the ballot, and register people to vote. Please note that the process is in two parts. The primary election in June and the general election in November.

| | | | |
|---|---|---|---|
| November General | Tuesday | 1/2/2018 | Earliest Independent candidate for November may file with GR or ELECT as appropriate for office sought |
| June Primary | Thursday | 3/29/2018 | 5 PM deadline for local office June primary candidates to file certificate of candidate qualification and, if applicable, statements of economic interests with his/her local general registrar and declaration, petitions and primary filing fee receipt with his/her local political party chairman |
| November General | Monday | 4/16/2018 | Deadline: Campaign Finance Report for Candidates on the ballot in November Election |
| June Primary | Friday | 4/27/2018 | Absentee voting for the June primary election must begin if absentee ballots were not sent previously |
| June Primary | Monday | 5/21/2018 | Last day to register to vote in the June Primary |
| June Primary | Saturday | 6/9/2018 | In-Person Absentee Voting - The general registrar's office shall be open a minimum of eight hours between the hours of 8:00 a.m. and 5:00 p.m. |
| June Primary | Tuesday | 6/12/2018 | Primary Day for November elections |
| November General | Monday | 7/16/2018 | Deadline: Campaign Finance Report for Candidates on the ballot in November Election |
| November General | Monday | 9/17/2018 | Deadline: Campaign Finance Report for Candidates on the ballot in November Election |
| November General | Monday | 10/15/2018 | Last day to register to vote in the November General election |

| | | | |
|---|---|---|---|
| November General | Monday | 10/15/2018 | Deadline: Campaign Finance Report for Candidates on the ballot in November election |
| November General | Saturday | 10/27/2018 | In-Person Absentee Voting - The general registrar's office shall be open a minimum of eight hours between the hours of 8:00 a.m. and 5:00 p.m. |
| November General | Monday | 10/29/2018 | Deadline: Campaign Finance Report for Candidates on the ballot in November election |
| November General | Saturday | 11/3/2018 | In-Person Absentee Voting - The general registrar's office shall be open a minimum of eight hours between the hours of 8:00 a.m. and 5:00 p.m. |
| November General | Tuesday | 11/6/2018 | November General Election Day |

(Virginia Department of Elections, 2018)

## Weekly Schedule

Your daily schedule should consist of doors and donors. A sample week would go as follows:

**<u>Breakfast 8:00-8:30</u>**

Make sure you eat something because you will need all the energy you can muster.

**<u>Call time Prep 8:30-9:00</u>**

Spend this time going over your call time strategy with your finance director.

**<u>Call time 9:00-12:00</u>**

You should be making at least 30 - 60 calls an hour.

**<u>Lunch 12:00-1:00</u>**

Take 30 minutes to eat and reset. Use the other thirty for political calls or interviews.

**<u>Call time 1:00-3:30</u>**

Keep grinding out those calls.

**<u>Travel to Turf 3:30-4:00</u>**

Grab your turf and get moving.

**4-8pm** Knock doors until dawn.



**<u>Canvass Launch 10:30-11:00</u>**

All your volunteers will meet you at a pre-determined location to receive their turf and follow- up instructions. Your field director should have already cut all the turf that you will need for the day.

**<u>Door knocking 11:00-1:30</u>**

Don't waste time at your canvass launch. Get people what they need and get to work.

**<u>Break 1:30-2:00</u>**

Reset, take a break and get ready for the long haul.

**<u>Door knocking 2:00-Finish</u>**

Knock doors until you hit your goal. Your personal goal should be 300-500 doors.

The volunteers should finish their turf and turn it in to your field director at the end of their shift.

Volunteers who do not want to knock doors can phone bank or assist with office work.



**<u>Churches 8:00-12:30</u>**

Sunday is primetime to visit churches. You can make it to at least three services if you're lucky (8:00, 10:30, 11:30). Your campaign manager should have called and scheduled your church visits at least a week ahead of time.

When you arrive, identify yourself and someone will help you. Some pastors will want to meet with you before the service starts so being early is paramount! The pastors will give you instructions on how to proceed.

Please note that some churches will not let you speak and if you are allowed, you will only have three minutes to address the congregation.

Don't pass out your literature without the express consent of the pastor or clergy. Many churches will not let you pass it out so don't be surprise if you are denied.

**<u>Door knocking 2:00-Finish</u>**

Get back out there and hit some more doors. More people are home on Sunday after church.

## June Primary

You will repeat your weekly schedule until late April - early May. In May, you will start dropping your mailers and you might have a debate. At the end of May, you will stop raising money and start raising votes during your get out the vote campaign.

The June primary is right around the corner and it is time to be direct with voters about them voting. When you call them, ask them to vote for you and ask them what their voting plan is. Some voters will vote absentee and others will vote in person. Make sure to convey to them the day, time, and place for their voting precinct. When you speak to a voter who says that their vote does not count, remember me. Tell them that I lost by 12 votes! Every vote counts!

## Election Day

You finally made it! Get up at 5:00 am and get ready for a long day of standing at the polls, shaking hands, and taking photos. Go to the polls and be the first one to vote for yourself. After you vote, stand outside 50 feet or more away from the building and meet and greet voters. There will be signs that advise you not to campaign beyond this point. Find a good spot and hand out sample ballots. Make sure that you thank everyone for coming out to vote. Most people who come out already know who they are going to vote for. However, some voters will come up to you and ask you why they should vote for you. Be prepared to answer all questions from your voters. Polls close at 7:00 pm, so pace yourself, stay hydrated, and have fun.

# After the Election

The numbers are in and hopefully you won! Thank all your family, volunteers, staff, and voters for supporting your campaign and remember to be humble. After you celebrate that night, you should take a day or so to reset because the fight will continue to November and you will work twice as hard to get elected.

If you lost your race, you have to regroup and support the winners. Remember that the race is not about you. It's about your constituents. You will have another chance to run again and you will need all the practice that you can get.

# Summer months

You are back for the long haul and it's time to get back to work. Stick to your daily schedule as much as possible. It is summer time and many voters are on vacation. Some are home and events are everywhere. Go to public events where the voters are and introduce yourself. Make sure to hit your doors but make time for your friends and family because at the end of summer, you will be fully committed to doors and donors. Remember that a campaign is a jog, not a sprint. You must find a work, life, campaign balance to maintain your spiritual health. Drink plenty of water and exercise at least twice a week.

# 4<sup>th</sup> Quarter

It's game time! September has arrived, and it's time to start dropping your literature in the voters' mailbox. The campaign is heating back up and you are hitting as many doors as you can. Your daily schedule will remain the same until GOTV. You will be working heavily with your mail firm to construct your mail. Make sure that your mailers speak to your constituents and not your party. You have been speaking with your voters for months and if you want them to vote for you, you must address their issues. You must convey to them that you will be their champion. Most people will not vote unless you give them a reason to. Voter turnout is low in most local races because most voters don't know that there is a race every year in Virginia. It is your responsibility to spread the word about yearly November elections.

## General Election Day

This is the final day of the election. It is no different than the primary election day. You will go vote and all your volunteers will be working the polls with you or knocking on doors to turnout voters.

## Thank You

I believe that it is important that we all do our civic duty to ensure that our children's lives are better than ours. My hope is that you have learned something that can help you be a better you so you can serve your community. Thank you from the bottom of my heart for reading my book. If you ever need assistance or have questions, feel free to contact by email at joshua.kingsr@gmail.com.

# Notes

# Works Cited


Actblue. (2018, July 6). *Features*. Retrieved from
Actblue.com: https://secure.actblue.com/features

Brian O'Day, J. (2018, June 6). *Political Campaign Planning
Manual.* Retrieved from National Democratic
Institute: https://www.ndi.org/sites/default/files/Afgh-
campaign-planning-manual-ENG.pdf

Duignan, B., & Plamenatz, J. (2018, June 2). *Jeremy-Bentham*.
Retrieved from ENCYCLOPÆDIA
BRITANNICA: https://www.britannica.com/biography/Jeremy-
Bentham

GreatSchools Staff. (2018, April 9). *What makes a great school board
member?* Retrieved from
Great!Schools.org:https://www.greatschools.org/gk/articles/wha
t-makes-a-great-school-board-member/

Herndon, A. W. (2018, June 21). *Democrats Plan New Effort to Target
Minority Voters.* Retrieved from The New York
Times: https://www.nytimes.com/2018/06/21/us/politics/demo
crats-minority-voters-midterms.html

*Karl Marx.* (2018, June 25). Retrieved
fromhttps://karlmarxradicalism.weebly.com/radicalism.html

Lauter, D. (2018, March 20). *Democratic, Republican voter bases are
more different than ever.* Retrieved from Los Angeles
Times: http://www.latimes.com/politics/la-na-pol-voter-groups-
20180320-story.html

Minogue, K., Girvetz, H., Dagger, R., & Ball, T. (2018, June
25). *Liberalism*. Retrieved from ENCYCLOPÆDIA
BRITANNICA: https://www.britannica.com/topic/liberalism

MRSC. (2018, February 27). *Roles and Responsibilities of Local
Government Leaders*. Retrieved from MRSC Local Government
Success: http://mrsc.org/Home/Explore-
Topics/Governance/Offices-and-Officers/Roles-and-
Responsibilities.aspx

NGP VAN. (2018, July 6). *Fundraising*. Retrieved from NGP VAN: https://www.ngpvan.com/feature/fundraising

*Philosophy Basics*. (2018, June 25). Retrieved from The Basics of Philosophy: https://www.philosophybasics.com/branch_conservatism.html

*Political Campaign Tips*. (2018, June 22). Retrieved from The Big List of Local Elected Offices for Political Candidates: http://www.politicalcampaigningtips.com/the-big-list-of-local-elected-offices-for-political-candidates/

Virginia Department of Elections. (2016, February 17). *Calendar*. Retrieved from Virginia Department of Elections:https://www.elections.virginia.gov/Files/Media/Calendar/2015_2019_Calendar.pdf

Virginia Department of Elections. (2018, June 26). Retrieved from Virginia Department of Elections:https://www.elections.virginia.gov/Files/Forms/Candidates/Petition-of-Qualified-Voters-SBE-506_521_letter.pdf

Virginia Department of Elections. (2018, June 1). *Becoming a Candidate*. Retrieved from Virginia Department of Elections: https://www.elections.virginia.gov/candidatepac-info/becoming-a-candidate/index.html

Virginia Department of Elections. (2018, July 9). *Calendars & Schedules*. Retrieved from Virginia Department of Elections: https://www.elections.virginia.gov/media/calendars-schedules/election-deadlines.html

Virginia Department of Elections. (2018, July 9). *Candidate Bulletins*. Retrieved from Virginia Department of Elections:https://www.elections.virginia.gov/Files/BecomingACandidate/CandidateBulletins/2018-11-06%20Gen%20&%20Sp%20Bulletin%20US%20House%20rev%201-10-18.pdf

Virginia Department of Elections. (2018, June 26). *Candidate Forms*. Retrieved from Virginia Department of

Elections: https://www.elections.virginia.gov/Files/Forms/Candidates/SBE_501_4-rev7-18.pdf

Virginia Department of Elections. (2018, June 26). *Update/check Voter Registration*. Retrieved from Virginia Department of Elections: https://www.elections.virginia.gov/voter-outreach/update-registration.html

VPAP. (2018, July 6). *About Us*. Retrieved from VPAP.org: https://www.vpap.org/about-us/mission/

VPAP. (2018, July 6). *King for Delegate*. Retrieved from VPAP.org: https://www.vpap.org/committees/264065/king-for-delegate-josh/

Wellstone. (2018, July 1). Retrieved from Wellstone.org:https://www.wellstone.org/sites/default/files/attachments/Campaign-Roles-and-Responsibilities_0.pdf